Awake at 3 a.m.

John Bartlett

Awake at 3 a.m.

Thanks

Thanks to all who supported this collection, above all Joan Fenney and members of my poetry group, especially Yvonne, Julie, Lyn and Wendy. Above all thanks to Stephen Matthews who gave me this opportunity to publish a full collection.

For Stephen, who sometimes lends me his eyes

Awake at 3 a.m.
ISBN 978 1 76041 975 2
Copyright © text John Bartlett 2020
Cover design: Ink to Screen

First published 2020 by
GINNINDERRA PRESS
PO Box 3461 Port Adelaide 5015
www.ginninderrapress.com.au

Contents

Awake at 3 a.m.	9
Vulnerability	10
Night	11
Absence & Presence	12
Once	13
Grace Still Hovers	14
What a piece of work is Man	15
Just Briefly	16
On God's watch	17
Gancho/Cortina	18
Transitioning	19
The Noumea Quartet	20
To you the guiltless	24
The Angelus	25
Danger	26
Waiting	27
Certainty	28
Listening for the past	29
Soldier love	30
Mistakes	31
Still surprised	32
Last Light	33
Shame	34
The city of recurring dreams	35
The Uncertainty of Men	36
Passion	37
Plastic world	38
Wet sparrows	39
Your Smile	40
The Suburbs	41

Drifting	42
Manus	43
Eloquence	44
In the shade of the acacia	45
Silvereye	46
Saying the Rosary	47
Jacaranda	48
Apocalypse	49
Some God	50
I lie down	51
Rewind	53
Insouciance	54
The Blue	55
Surprised by Love	56
The poet at work	57
Red Brick Wall	59
Bridge Road	60
47 Alison Street, 1984	61
Litanies on the Homeward Road	62
Lower Murray Nungas Club	64
The wedding dress	65
Remembering Michaell	66
Surf Coast, Boxing Day 2015	67
Surfers – Pt Impossible	68
Powerplay	69
Damaged Angels	70
Reflections on oblivion	71
Herons	73
Barre Warre – from the hills to the sea	74
Rattling doors	75
A World Full of Things	76
Outside the flags	77

Winter thoughts	79
Past Goodbyes	80
Time	81
My brief affair	82
The Beloved is Mine	83
Mother shepherd	84
God, my Father	85
Out of the depths I cry…	86
Cast-off	87
She Saw Two Girls and a Boy, 1966	88
Still Waiting	91
Warnings	92
One goodbye	93
In the steps of Eugenio	95
Exclusion	99
O Res Mirabilis	102
Misunderstanding Good Friday	103
Life is	104
Friendly Fire	105
The call of the Border	106
The falcon	107
Tenderness	108
Still around	109
Close encounters with headlines	110
My Acolyte Eyes	112
Lizard	113
Disturbed by zinnias	114
Bella Donna	115
Wetlands	116
The McDonald's Car Park Massacre	117
The ambiguity of hands	118
Mind the gap	119

Domesticated Violence	120
Holding on to the Bible	121
Small matters	122
Hope	123
After the surgery	124
Love letter to the Führer	126
Self-portrait by Berthe Morisot	127
A Ghazal	128
Know thyself	129
Acknowledgements	130
Poems Appearing in *The Arms of Men*	132

Awake at 3 a.m.

The night releases secrets
the day knows nothing of –
Vespers notes are fading,
murmuring muted mantras
apologetically,
dissonant dreams colliding.

God made this lesser light
to rule the night,
to seed regret and shame,
those casualties of love,
to strike mute
all guarding angels
stranded here below in doubt.

Be still, await
the shy light of morning,
this greater light
to rule the day,
until the crystal-throated Matins
of guiltless magpies
sound the all-clear.

Vulnerability

The white porcelain cup cracks
A hummingbird trapped in a box
We balance on high wires
At 18 he hanged himself

A hummingbird trapped in a box
Fire ignites in locked rooms
At 18 he hanged himself
We pace the floor for answers

Fire ignites in locked rooms
Desire flares like embers in treetops
We pace the floor for answers
Colours tremble on stone floors

Desire flares like embers in treetops
Emotion a hound slipped its leash
Colours tremble on stone floors
The sea alone is forgiving

Emotions a hound slipped its leash
Our sins multiply on scoreboards
The sea alone is forgiving
The white porcelain cups cracks

Night

Night falls too early now
Birds fold themselves up
Like faded Christmas cards

Clocks speed up their complaining
Cars creep towards home
Fog like a smoker's cough

Friends leave through the open door
Coats and scarves are left behind
The beach washed clear of footprints

We wait in darkened rooms
Voices calling in the distance
A choir of galloping angels

Absence & Presence

Wrens sing
notes trickling sideways
insects shout out rudely

the absent-minded dung beetle
keeps excavating while
hairy cicadas
serenade each other
silently

cows float in amber paddocks
the sun a hovering seductress

but you still absent.

Once

Mictyris longicarpi
in blue jackets
burrowed into mudflats
where *Naticidae*
drilled into sea snail shells
dining on soft flesh,
where timid prawns
shivered
in mangrove swamps
Now
the Eastern curlew
flies 10,000 ks
to find
Ocean View – location
and lifestyle opportunity
where dust flies up from
trucks of ready-mix concrete,
no job too big
Curlews circling

Grace Still Hovers

The swan
in clerical black
raises her head
above the nest
with crosiered care.

The cleric
lifts up the knife
for infanticide
dripping blood
down altar steps.

The tabernacle
has been ransacked,
angels sob
in deserted cloisters.
Assassins dwell
within the gates.

The swan glides,
sculpting the water
with her memories,
cygnets attached
like an umbilical cord.
The cob follows behind
attentive,
alert for predators.

Grace still hovers
over the earth.

What a piece of work is Man

You are too old to look at men like that
to leer, to stare, to bare their bodies with your eyes,
to dream like young men do, of
cock, of arse, of balls and all the rest
that burns away one's will.

You should be ashamed
to put your mouth on lips or taste
the curve of arse and heft of cock,
the salt of groin and pit,
to feel those arms go round and hold.

Just Briefly

We need your babies
your infants & your teens
to fill our prison cells.

You see
we spent all your money
on new facilities
with shiny bars
and sparkly cages
but criminals are no longer
recidivist enough.

So
we need your babies
to fill our quotas
and
to stop them crying
we may dose them with
Olanzapine
or
Duloxetine
just briefly
to justify the new facilities
using your money.

Thank you
for your attention.

On God's watch

She looked at life
through a porthole
my mother,
at clouds,
puffed up with care,
at God's eye,
looking back at her.

What kept her going
were roses and her children,
the living and the lost ones.

Afternoons in that cane chair,
nodding in sunlight,
newspaper and glasses
discarded at your feet,
God seemed
a little kinder

Gancho/Cortina

(inspired by words from *Twelve Minutes of Love: A Tango Story* by Kapka Kassabova)

With longing we begin
as strangers,
longing that is full of trouble,
longing for what
we can never have.
Still we embrace
for a moment,
we can't help it,
then separate,
out of danger at last,
but still
full of longing.

In the end
longing is being
on your own.

Transitioning

Some days I'm a
drag queen careering
on roller skates
with fireworks exploding
from my hair.
Get out of the way,
I'm a hand grenade
about to pull the pin.
I smoke like a coal-fired power station
and don't give a shit.
I wind up the windows
when I see charity collectors
at traffic lights,
Nights
I sit in dark rooms
and shout at the TV.
Other days,
I fold myself up
neatly into small boxes
I remember to put out the bins
I draw in straight lines
and I'm polite to phone marketers.
I'm just
transitioning.

The Noumea Quartet

1 The glittering Pacific

I woke up in the hotel Beaurivage,
the waves of the glittering Pacific
smaller than I expected.
Kanak mothers
rinsing babies in the sea
like bundles of dirty laundry.

We wallowed in the curve
of the Baie de Citrons.
What seemed essential
slipped away,
sim cards now irrelevant,
my schoolboy French
suddenly adequate.

The sun on pale skin,
the resting tide rippling
across stones.
You and I together,
the universe tilting
in our general direction.

2 The Women of Noumea

The women of Noumea
glide by
on clouds of sangfroid
limbs moving
like champagne
in tall glasses,
feet gliding effortlessly
like roller skaters,
hair set free
like yachts
scudding
across the Baie de Citrons,
faces sculpted
from black marble,
dredged up from sea beds,
a glistening *mulier fortis*.

…and oh,
how you love your children.

3 Madonna of the Baie de Citrons

Outside the hotel Beaurivage
she paces out an ancient vigil,
muttering self-taught prayers.

The bus she waits for
will not arrive.
She's consecrated
to the lights
that simmer round the bay,
beads on a dangling rosary.

I close the curtains
on those long night hours,
her compassionate companions.

Then,
at the quiet light
of morning
she stands at water's edge,
the *flêche faitiere*,
guiding home the souls
of departed family.

One passing sparrow
calls out her name
in recognition.

4 Time Passes

In Rue Auguste Brun
dusty glass cases
hold headdresses eons old,
their feathers painting
the shaded stillness of
a New Caledonia afternoon.

Doors spring open
releasing Kanak children
with hair like electric spaghetti
'Come back after lunch'
says the dreadlocked doorman
'You don't have time
to see it all now.'

We step back into
Rue Auguste Brun
where time slows to a trickle,
women in flowered dresses
chat under
lipstick pink bougainvillea.

Time, callous and blind,
dismisses my small life
like a rejecting lover.

To you the guiltless

Savage winds still unsettle the guiltless
Rippling trees bear coded messages
While travellers await updated messages
White roses cascade through our memories.

Rippling trees bear coded messages
Your grave, alas, has no tombstone
White roses cascade through our memories.
I've waited too long for your call.

Your grave, alas, has no tombstone
Our memories will vanish like vapour
I've waited too long for your call.
Counting extra days on both hands

Our memories will vanish like vapour
Clocks ticking blindly at night
Counting extra days on both hands
All will be well at the end

Clocks ticking blindly at night
I move quietly down dark hallways
All will be well at the end
Savage winds still unsettle the guiltless

The Angelus

Bring back the Angelus –
unhurried song of heaven,
distilled voice of God,
announcing
events undreamed of.

This is not all there is
and
none of this will last.

Long before final notes falter,
lingering across valleys,
sinking into shadows,
your cortège will creep
like a small, black beetle
across the vast landscape
of a wrinkling leaf.

The Angelus forever silent.

Danger

A knife in a drawer full of spoons
Smiles unsheathed like swords
Dangers lurk in the bottom of your glass

Outside the door marauding tigers
A tea bag might strangle you
A lawnmower take revenge

Sharks tread water patiently at beaches
Even serial killers queue at libraries
Assassins lurk in every shadow

Why bother getting up in the morning?
The cat might break your leg
But there's something truly compelling about living
Even if it's all over just too soon.

Waiting

Clouds wait patiently for sunsets
Trees long for life from an artist's brush
A hand hovers over the pause button
A waiting world walks back and forth

Trees long for life from an artist's brush
At times the earth rotates more slowly
A waiting world walks back and forth
Birds now losing their way home

At times the earth rotates more slowly
In the streets dizzy crowds assembling
Birds now losing their way home
Sometimes we need a new agenda

In the streets dizzy crowds assembling
On a corner a preacher shouts at god
Sometimes we need a new agenda
Messiahs are going out of business

On a corner a preacher shouts at god
A hand hovers over the pause button
Messiahs are going out of business
Clouds wait patiently for sunsets

Certainty

If a leaf falls from a tree.
someone is tossed by nightmares.

If a single note sounds in an empty hall,
a fault-line cracks under the ocean.

If a tiny bird settles on a branch,
a child's dream comes true.

If you lose your way on a dark road,
someone surfs the perfect wave.

As a rose unfurls its perfection,
an old man dies alone.

When the sea roars at night,
somewhere there are tears.

And,

If you hold someone,
you love them.

Listening for the past

Listening for the past
is no way to spend an afternoon
when boats scud across windy bays,
families ricocheting around parks,
speeded up days.

Yet I still hear
my mother in a kitchen
flooded with the smell of baking scones
listening to *Portia Faces Life*
from a cracked Bakelite near the kettle.

My whistling father
bending over strawberry beds,
bees buzzing in blue salvia.

Or I hear too much silence
in empty college chapels,
the whack of leather straps
on young boys' hands,
their stifled sobs at night.
The past is unpredictable –
a country of smudged memories

Soldier love

what if soldiers fucked each other
tenderly
instead of shooting the enemy
quickly?

caressed each other's gleaming limbs
slowly
instead of disembowelling the enemy
in one red second?

what if soldiers just kissed each other
on the lips
tasted each other's panic and loneliness?

or fondled each other's
legs, chests, nipples, arses
caressed each other's fear
until morning broke?

what if soldiers fucked each other
instead of fucking the enemy
and really   liked it?

then they might start
loving the enemy too

Mistakes

Tea tree flowers mistaken for snow
A bird on an aimless afternoon
How much time is left to me
And why are you walking ahead?

A bird on an aimless afternoon
Clouds gather like bargain hunters
And why are you walking ahead?
Time is an advancing avalanche.

Clouds gather like bargain hunters
Rain prepares to change its mind
Time is an advancing avalanche
Weather a recalcitrant child.

Rain prepares to change its mind
Days like an absent family
Weather a recalcitrant child
Counting the hours on both hands now.

Days like an absent family
Sea alone belongs to me
Counting the hours on both hands now
Tea tree flowers mistaken for snow.

Still surprised

The Paris train creeps
across the Camargue wetlands
a cathedral rising slowly
from a deserted beach
where a black dog
chases a yellow ball
and leadlighted saints wink
at observant passengers.

There are still surprises
for those who dare to breath
on the glimmering coals of hope.
Your arms reach out
to lift me closer to your heart.

There are surprises still in store
for those who disembark
at Gare du Nord

Last Light

Light rushes to the west
clouds lose their bearings
We clutch at last light
before night rushes in
A silver artery
dissects the wetlands
Swans fold up their wings
reluctantly
Ducks drifting seaward
surrendering to creek swell
Longings stir in the deepest self
we are the seabirds
snatched by invisible rapture
abandoned to wind's whim
nonchalant in our desires
Nature tolerates no conscience

Shame

Let tides untie my deep desires,
retreating waves reveal my shameful dreams.
The roar of surf cannot erase
past deeds so badly done.

My crimes fly all around me
like startled crows in fright.
My guilt and shame,
the signs I tried,
but often failed to be
the man I thought I was.

The city of recurring dreams

I dreamt I saw a city's
skyscrapers simmering on the horizon
like a child's misplaced toy
still afloat
but sinking resolutely
under the weight of self opinion
Confused
I wondered
which was north and south

Truth after all
is just a collection
of recurring dreams

The Uncertainty of Men

Arms
more used to wielding heavy weapons,
reach out
to hold me.

Lips
more used to giving orders
search for mine
in silence.

Men
more used to bearing arms
adept at rape & pillage
sometimes reach out,
desire stripped raw
war postponed
for now.

Leaking tenderness,
you lie in my embrace
defenceless
for now
arms around each other
I'm wounded by your longing.

Or,
am I embracing
an unexploded anger
our intimacy
collateral damage?

Passion

The unmapped pathways
of passion reignited
seduce me still.

The curves of
hidden tracks,
lead to deserts
where explorers before me
have perished.

Passion is a foreboding journey,
the push and pull of it,
the once trusted compass
spinning out of control.

Desire flings up
such haughty beauties,
obsession
such casual deceits

Plastic world

It hardly matters
there's a cellophane wrapper
or a plastic bag or two
blowing along the street,
plastic clouds filling up the sky
and blue-grey plastic light
covering the world in non-recyclable mist.

The world is turning plastic.

It hardly matters
there's a plastic bottle or two
or two hundred billion
rattling down the roads
clogging up the world
and the whales are wearing plastic
this summer on their heads

The world is turning plastic

It hardly matters
the beach is sprouting
hypodermic needles

It hardly matters now.
The world is turning plastic.
Hardly.

Wet sparrows

(inspired by a line from *The Enlightenment of the Greengage Tree* by Shokoofeh Azar)

The wet sparrows are silent
deities scatter like skittish ponies
light disperses the hidden shadows
my heart-padlock is undone

Deities scatter like skittish ponies
that old god has gone AWOL
my heart-padlock is undone
life stretches like an unrolling carpet

That old god has gone AWOL
the tabernacle door is ajar
life stretches like an unrolling carpet
freedom is an arrow hurtling

The tabernacle door is ajar
churches burning & ransacked
freedom is an arrow hurtling
no pathway leads homeward

Churches burning & ransacked
hope still glows in the window
no pathway leads homeward
the wet sparrows are silent

Your Smile

Your smile
cracked open the carapace
around the heart
I'd been
defending,
strengthening,
protecting
against the tricks
of cruel desire,
so opportunistic
so unforgiving.

How could this small moment
subvert
my best laid plans?

The Suburbs

Overnight
the suburbs creep,
huddling mushrooms
with their grey roofs
and sense of entitlement
rhizomes tunnelling
through our dreams and our memories.

Across windswept paddocks
plastic bags prance
like iced-up free-range chooks.
disembowelled mattresses sprawl
abandoned near railways tracks
(where else?)
obscene remnants
of trickle-down economics.

Developers circle
in their purring Lamborghinis
like patient birds of prey.

Drifting

the air was full
of silences
sheep like
cardboard cut-outs
tattered & abandoned
trains creeping
guiltily
across an empty plain
onshore
the thwack of leather
on cricket bats
a prime minister
cheerily
tweeting scores,
offshore
the crack of clubs
on flesh
while no one was watching
the Ship of State
drifting
towards the rocks

Manus

These boy-men
are
still learning to be men
fleeing
the club
the lash
the gun
once more
controlled
contained
kept-boys
caged-boys
not-free-range-boys
bashed-boys
prisoner-of-war-boys
rabbits-in-traps-boys
not-yet-men-boys
but
caring-for-each-other
kind-boys
these
comrades-in-arms
these men-boys

And we
citizens of Salo

staring

Eloquence

The leaping eloquence
of the heart
desire like a post-hole digger
and you slipping through
a closing doorway.

My beloved's messages
are indecipherable.

How many beloveds
are you permitted
in one lifetime?

In the shade of the acacia

You were a procession of one
the day you first walked
in the shade of the acacia.

You were the Flores de Mayo
as you walked
in the shade of the acacia.

Branches applauded overhead
as I watched you walk
in the shade of the acacia.

You spoke an unfamiliar language
while I hesitated
less fluent than you in love
in the shade of those acacia.

Night softened the edges
around our shared loneliness
just the music of round stones
embracing themselves
at the tide's edge.

My treason was to leave you
to walk on alone
in the shade of the acacia.

Silvereye

I could spend my life
watching silvereye bathing,
the plunge and flight,
the delight of light
on droplets exploding.

Nearby branches trembling,
they queue for landing
like 747s at Heathrow
but patient, not urgent,
no timetable to meet,
they preen, absorbing
the slow hum of evening
then flit into twilight
leaving
an imprint of stillness.

Saying the Rosary

Each night we knelt, we four
held tight within the circle of the rosary
fingering our way through mysteries,
the joys, the sorrows of our saviour
speeding up the final 'glory bes',
accelerating, arriving just in time
for *News on Seven*.

The family that prays together, stays
together until the rosary snaps,
as needs it must, beads scattered
each *remember when* and *how was it when*
dispersed, stories dispensed with,
lives fading to translucent, then gone.

How brief we were a family,
how short the chance to love
until I alone abandoned,
the unreliable guardian
of stories my family told me.
Once broken, rosaries
are mere beads,
not blessings.

But still I do recall
that glorious mystery of
my father in his shed
bent over from telling stories,
his hands mending broken rosaries

Jacaranda

That November
we floated through the streets of Adelaide
in a celestial haze of jacaranda.

Outside the church
my car waited impatiently
in its pale mauve garment.

Inside, your coffin hovered,
preparing for its lift-off
while we trawled through
our memories of you
as if our acts of remembering
might impel you
to return.

Apocalypse

I once saw Gaddafi dying
on a Samsung wide-screen
while waiting at the New Hong Kong
for pork and plum sauce
with four steamed dim sims.

In aisle four at Safeway
searching for Indian pickles
my iPhone announced
refugees streaming out of Syria
clutching bloodied babies, clothes on fire.

Down on platform nine
we lined up like glittering soldiers.
Someone announced the Apocalypse was late,
signal failure down the line.
Luxury car ads flowed on a perennial loop,
sponsors mouthing cheery messages, like
mouths of vacant clowns, accelerating.

Some God

The long nights of being alone
stretch grey-dawned
fear-filled in a sea of strangers' faces

The whimpering soul
cringing in its back streets, garbage-strewn
searches for the friend's face
panic rising in the throat like bile

In tasting comes to know
the self that lies within
For at depth
each of us is alone
an island separate to itself
and only in that depth
can truly find some god

For they are to be pitied more
who have never been alone
nor in icy sweat
tramped the slums of the soul
and there
found some god

I lie down

At night I lie down
and dream of love,
wrapped tight
in the muscled arms of men.

On crowded railway platforms
men with olive skin
smile at me with green eyes.

In low-lit back streets
men in linen suits
pass me messages,
written on café napkins,
stained with red wine
or is it blood?

A man with hair alive
like electric snakes
passes close to me,
touches my elbow, then
stands in a doorway waiting,
his breath on my neck.

Men stamped with tattoos
of skulls and knives
whisper in my ear words
that can never be understood.

Love is a perilous country.
Innuendo lurks everywhere.

I still remember the orange sunlight
scorched in strips across white sheets
and your limbs arranged,
an impassable mountain range,
the humid air carrying promises
of kisses more articulate than words

Rewind

Over there
young men wrap themselves in flags
and suicide on sunny days
in outdoor cafes
spreading pink mist
over *soupe du jour*.

Here
arching jasmine stars
explode white
perfumed hope over bluestone walls
leading possibility by the hand
of re-attaching torn limbs
excavating coffins
from muddy graves
allowing tears to defy gravity
run back up cheeks
return to weeping eyes
while candles unburn
returning wax to bees
in fact
putting the whole fucking world on rewind
then creeping softly from the room
closing the door behind.

Insouciance

The young stroll by with insouciance
liquid limbs like wine in a glass
indifferent to casual spillages
conversations like
failed experiments in clarity,
they are
unstoppable blue wrens
bouncing from one search to the next
oblivious to dangers.
How enviable

The Blue

The blue of the ocean snatched up by sky
Fog smudges this perfect landscape
I wait to be called by name
The violinist on the street oblivious

Fog smudges this perfect landscape
Apple trees glow like stop lights
The violinist on the street oblivious
As children sleep, buried in dreams

Apple trees glow like stop lights
Crowds surge like advancing tides
As children sleep, buried in dreams
The sea drifts on with no guilt

Crowds surge like advancing tides
Somewhere a single gull complains
The sea drifts on with no guilt
A small boat on a vast canvas

Somewhere a single gull complains
I wait to be called by name
A small boat on a vast canvas
The blue of the ocean snatched up by sky

Surprised by Love

We scurry down-faced,
burdened by bin-bulk,
screen-glazed eyes intent,
bent to task,
till you, beloved,
lurking out of reach,
burst like fireworks,
scattering trivial pursuits.
You ignite body-shock,
star-burst in souls, light-switch flick,
in a dark room,
match-scratch to kindling
flaming, then devouring.

Do not fear
You are loved

The poet at work

1

Peer through my window
and what do you see?
Knock on my door,
is there anyone home?
A stained teacup in the sink,
a pot plant wilting in the corner.
I have no time for triviality.
My life cannot be measured
in putting out the bins.
I, the poet, too busy
at the desk,
shaping important words to outlive this life.

2

But when you speak,
the sun smashed through the windows,
and chased fear down the passageway,
like debris in a willy-willy.

Our ears ate up the crumbs of your words,
as we leant at dangerous angles in our chairs,
drunk on words that really mean something,
like drought breaking over dusty paddocks.

Unused to hearing real speech,
clubbed senseless by moneyspeak,
your words hurt and wound us,
knives plunged into soft bellies.

Your words have consequences,
Disturb and unsettle.
Now we feel unbalanced,
adrift in our rocking little dinghies.

Your words should have a price on their head.

Red Brick Wall

I've not scaled the heights of Machu Picchu,
dizzied and breathless, gazing
down the valley of the Urumbala.

When the sun set like a peach over Byzantium,
I was not there, sipping icy Chablis,
on the deck of a wandering yacht.

I lingered in the backyard,
under the Hills hoist,
idly bouncing a tennis ball,
against a red brick wall in Brunswick,
waiting to be summoned by the wondrous.

Bridge Road

It's two o'clock in Melbourne
when the sheltered workshops close their doors
pouring giggling workers onto slip-wet streets,
groups of bouncing acrobatic cherubs,
fingering the air at impatient Indian tram drivers,
jangling down Bridge Road,
guzzling their lives like orange juice,
dribbling innocence down blue-check shirtfronts
their insolent fingers like stop signs
while the tram drivers dream of nights
in perfumed Mumbai.

47 Alison Street, 1984

Strata Title – only two left
is what remains of number 47
Alison Street, where aged six
I put my arm round grandma
in the front garden.

Machines of demolition
scrape all away,
yet love has soaked this earth,
and Eulalie with plaited hair
bends over her students'
piano-ed hands
to the tick-tock of the metronome.

The pungent fruity smell
of pelargonium still
fills the air,
and despite brand new strata titles
I watch Celeste in
wedding ivory satin
step light of foot
into Alison Street in 1938.

Litanies on the Homeward Road

On the homeward road
my parents' voices batting
softly back and forth
like the litany of saints imploring
in the Holy Redeemer church,
Crafers, Stirling, all ye holy hills,
Bridgewater, pray for us.

Hahndorf – all ye blessed towns,
your curving, cradling arms,
Mt Barker – all ye holy innocents,
can Callington be far away,
where ghosts of miners
sleep in slaty beds?
Pray for us ye holy workers.

We climb White's Hill
where wandering spirits
search for homes below.
Holy river pray for us.
Almost home, almost asleep,
we speed the arrowed road
past my family's tombs,
where angels cry their sandstone tears,
cast flowers that never fall to earth,
tender movements, aspic-held.
All ye holy forebears, pray for us.

As my father lifts me from the car,
I'm dreaming, yet awake, contained,
in these strong arms of his
and in that movement, I'm
indelibly stamped with the desire
to be held forever
in the arms of men

Lower Murray Nungas Club

On one side of the road
where traffic growls
a damaged angel drops her marble flowers
over my elders William and Catherine
reunited in their cracked concrete bed.

William cut stone and felled timber
from Ngarrindjeri land
to supply a city expanding by the sea.
He grew rich and solid too.

On the other side of that road
the Ngarrindjeri tell stories and laugh
pulling all their strands together
into tight baskets.

I'm straddling that road,
trying to keep a foot in both camps.

I think the Nungas Club is winning

The wedding dress

We spread your wedding dress
beside you in your coffin
a gown of ivory satin, the skirt
flared from the waist, merging into a train.

You lie in your favourite floral pink
best walking shoes on sturdy ankles
handbag with half a packet of soft jubes
to chew along the way

We cannot believe
that you have gone
and will walk with us
no more in these gardens

We are the ones who are lost now
while you walk on
without your walking frame
under the shade of Moreton Bay figs

Remembering Michaell

This morning I saw you again at Circular Quay –

You were the old woman in plaid shorts
her grey hair sprawling like mist about her face
and her stick tapping the ground ahead.

The young boy, skipping and giggling
between his mother with a pram
and a sister in pink chiffon.

The young man in the ticket office
bellowing a hearty *good morning*
to anyone who cared to notice.

There were bits of you everywhere
glinting in the sunlight of this
simmering Sydney morning.

And your arm I felt around my shoulders
as we crossed the harbour one more time,
made tiny under the arch
of that confident steel embrace
which links all we journeyers together
connecting, always connecting

Surf Coast, Boxing Day 2015

Sketched upon the cartridge
of this morning's beach
wavering charcoal lines
searching for a story
scribbled by retreating tides.

Leaves, bark chips, small pieces of blackened timber
not quite destroyed
just baked in one explosive curse
of fire and angry flames.

Charred too at the edges
are memories
of long summer afternoons
of tinkling glasses on shaded verandas
of laughter and of children's voices
echoing in the dunes
of watching kookaburras,
voyeurs on tall branches.

These private moments too
sucked into the furnace
reduced to ash
wind-blown now
across the sand.

'You only live once'
laughed the man with the blue surfboard
as he strode across the ash-strewn beach
to where the patient sea
still waited.

Surfers – Pt Impossible

Etched black on a sullen sea
sainted statues adoring seaward
silent expectation in
one clean cone of concentration

this pause
before the earth revolves again.

Powerplay

The statues of the gods
need polyfilla to
repair embarrassing cracks.

Thrones rust the same as surfers' utes,
bumping down corrugated tracks at dawn.

Presidential proclamations can leak
like party balloons

And even papal motorcades
sometimes get flat tyres

Queens in gilded carriages
might have to get out and push

Privilege is a brown snake
in a woodpile,
dangerous and deadly if provoked

Damaged Angels

An archangel a little damaged,
a God past his use-by date.
Nothing is really perfect any more.

I saw the Mother of God once
serving take-away in a restaurant
on the edge of the Nullarbor,
and the sky such a perfect blue,
a day made in heaven you said
and she, trying to pay the rent.

God got pulled over once,
sprung over .05,
coming home from an angel convention
or so he said, with breath
smelling of cask wine
and clothes of cheap perfume.

These days the sky is full of falling bodies,
thudding rain upon the roofs,
a smell of burning feathers.

Reflections on oblivion

1 Memories are not enough

Memories are
translucent
transparent
and by winds blown away.
Nor are concrete mausoleums enough
after a thousand years of wind and rain.

I want an edge on permanence
when it comes to eternity
and even though
childless
I will not be forgotten
when all vanishes in smoke.

Saying 'I will not'
is enough for now

2 Memorabilia

I still drive by there when I visit that city where I grew up. I'm not sure what to expect after so long. Will there be changes? The fence is still sagging where Dad planted the wisteria. He's been gone more than forty years now but his camellia is still a shocking pink against the red brick wall where Mum and Dad posed for that photo before I left for overseas. The little black and white photo curled at the edges where it's been resting in the drawer with that box of other memorabilia, I brought home after going through Mum's things.
What's worth remembering and what's worth forgetting?

My father comes to me from a garden, overgrown with roses. He called his roses 'circus' roses but I never heard anybody else call them that. Colours were like a circus, red and yellow, like a tumbling clown. Made you catch your breath like a high-wire flight.
Worth remembering colours like these.
Memories blow away like ash; as we struggle to remember we become dust ourselves.
Why should anyone still remember when we have stopped our own remembering?
Long after I'm gone, the ragged wisteria will still thrust itself rudely through a broken fence demanding to be seen.
Things worth remembering are too ephemeral to survive.
Things worth remembering will not survive.
Even my remembering will not be remembered.

Herons

A heron on the rocks
beak poised for fishing.
Everything in its place,
except for you.

So while I was noticing herons
and my back was turned,
you slipped away
and herons kept fishing.

Barre Warre – from the hills to the sea

From the hills to the sea
from those heaven-hugging You Yangs to the east
they journeyed to the Karafe wetlands behind Pt Impossible
when the shearwater laid eggs in burrow nests
they sat in soft hollows of breasted-dunes
on shell-fish feasted – kooderoo, moorabool, barrabool
on low fires roasted – dora, yabbi and wiitji
the names still echo in the dunes like prayers
their soft footprints in the sand
erased now by the 'Sands Development'
eighteen-hole golf course and sleek condominiums rising
from the wetlands
where red-eyed bulldozers blink in the dust
whingeing-whining seven days a week
with bunkers, greens and a clubhouse
covering the tracks of those Wathaurong
forever gone.

Rattling doors

Today's a day of rattling doors.
The wind perhaps
or you just out of reach,
your shadow vanishing
around the corner of my mind?

A World Full of Things

An empty street and our house for sale
A lamb's weak bleat and a whale's song

A plate of rice and a nail that's bent
A head full of lice and a room for rent

Birds in a cage and a traffic jam
A wife in a rage and a leaking dam

Chicken with spice and a kangaroo
A wife being nice and a cow's sad moo

A white-hot beach and a clouded moon
A long boring speech and a bursting balloon

A madman loose and a high thick wall
The hangman's noose or a baby's first crawl

A door ajar and a flag at half-mast
A distant star and your neck in a cast

A car stuck in mud and a lover's caress
A bucket of blood and a wedding dress

Which do you think are my favourite things?

Outside the flags

I met you on a Surfcoast beach
where the hooded plover breeds
that beach where
when people approach a nest the parent plover leaves
chicks and eggs vulnerable to scavengers like gulls, foxes and cats
just six hundred hooded plovers left

They're a threatened species it seems
and so are you,
you children from East Timor, Afghanistan, Somalia, Eritrea,
Ethiopia, Sudan and Iraq
just chicks and eggs

You rushed down our beach as if you'd never seen the sea before
Elias had already seen a different sea
journeyed all the way from Nazaria in Iraq
aged 17 through Malaysia, Indonesia
saw his sea from a leaky boat
Nazaria to Woomera
'We came for freedom' you said
but 'it was sad'

Some of the girls wore hijab
climbed over black volcanic rocks, spewed from nearby Mt Duneed
in a lava stream a million years old
looking like large heron birds
the same pale mauve of their hijab against the black rocks
searching in the pools between the rocks
like heron
searching for freedom

You offered me your lunch
as if I was the guest
on your shores
I've never tasted halal sausages before, I said

Brother and sister, Elvis and Erna
torn from East Timor seven years ago
sat on that beach and shared dreams
rooted here now and putting out new growth
Elvis seventeen on a springboard to university
Erna, fifteen dreaming of sports medicine

Today I hear that
Elvis is now permanent and may stay with us
but Erna and her family will likely be sent back
nicely sliced down the middle this family
future uncertain it seems

That day we taught you about
sea safety and swimming between the flags
how rips can suddenly drag you out to sea
pity
you were all swimming
outside the flags

Winter thoughts

Solitary

Late-night talk radio
Blows across empty car parks
Music bounces off frosted windows
A voice tunnels through dark alleys.
What if nobody is listening?

Tradition

I stand on ice
How thick I do not know
Embedded in tradition
Solid and cold
Feet thick or inches
Does it matter if I do not know?

First steps

First class
Standing against the back fence
Covered in Lorraine Lee rose
One foot thrust forward ready to meet the world
And you my brother about to leave me
To my own resources
At the age of five

Past Goodbyes

An express train
Blurs through an empty station
Scatters memories of stale goodbyes
Some drift to earth
But most float away
Forever forgotten.

Time

Morning knocks on my door politely
Two Mormons in dark shiny suits.

Midday is a rude foot in the door

And night like an argument,

Sudden,
Bitter,
And unexpected.

My brief affair

Was it love at first glance
when your knee-touch first singed
my waiting thighs, widening,

my eyes unbuttoning
your shy desire,
my eager thoughts opening
your zippered smile,

your cold eyes resisting
my bold'ning stare,
your stiff arms excluding
my bursting heart,

until stop sixty-nine
when you abandoned me
without a backward glance?

And so ended
my brief affair.

The Beloved is Mine

We touch like two sliding
deckchairs
on the *Titanic*'s raked deck.
One quick embrace
sucks me down into green warm sea.
I hold back.
Body won't go where mind lingers.
All you want is our embrace now.
I stroke your arms and legs.
You arch toward me,
you kiss my mouth,
you drown yourself in me.
It frightens me this power
that draws you in.
There in you
I drown too.
We go down together.

Mother shepherd

Stretching, slowly snaking,
the chord that ties and binds.
The further you run,
the more it stretches,
pulls you back to my breasts
with poisoned milk of love.

Suck on, into suffocation,
while I wrap you in these arms
that pour forth only good things.
You can't escape
my forceps-arms,
which pull you from the womb.
My child born out of time.

Got you now.
You are mine,
my child, flesh of my flesh.
Forever you will pay the price.

This shepherd's love protects
with soft pillows,
across the mouth.

You are mine,
preserved forever,
embalmed,
on the shrine of love.
The smiling innocent,
snared behind glass,
trapped in a silver frame.
'Oh, hasn't he got his mothers' eyes.'

God, my Father

Stumbling down dark corridors
where strangers surge and ebb
washed in from some dark sea
they loom and fade,
neon-like
but none the face I seek.
We speak
not to one another
but eyes search eyes
yearning for a spark
to light a lamp,
and lead us out of this mazed gloom.
Perhaps it is my father
I seek
sleepwalking
outside his tomb?
We both have trouble with farewells
you and I
but now I think
I can see why.
The child grows bigger
and needs room to run
but still looks back
from whence he's come.
For even in the adult
who strides ahead
lurks the child
who would cling longer.

Out of the depths I cry…

'You say, "This is my body"
You raise high the pure white host
for all to see.
No, this is your body,
throbbing and trembling in its shame
with its passions and its lusts aflame.
This is your body,
keeping silent vigil
with itself
on nights like this alone.
Your body is not made
of pure white bread,
but mixed
with mouldy flour
and you lie,
dashed-down in utter frailty.
But it is your body.
Embrace it
as Jesus did his own.
And be not afraid.
Your body
is held tight
in my arms,
safe, secure,
so sleep little one, sleep.'

Cast-off

San Nicholas in silk and precious robes
is lifted high above the heads
of peasant farmers
with gnarled and dirt-scrubbed hands.
Their clothes have lost their colour
from too many washes
against smooth stones in the river.
San Nicholas is leering down at them
and loving it
Why have you cast us off?
Why have you dashed us against the stones?

She Saw Two Girls and a Boy, 1966

after a photo by Melbourne photographer Polixeni Papapetrou
(for my mother)

1

She saw two girls and a boy
while waiting for the tram at Glenelg beach.
She knew they were her own,
that's the age they'd be by now.
The moment shimmered on pause
until she saw the tram turning into Jetty road
and scrambled in her purse for change.
To strangers' eyes they looked not real
just papier mâché models, expressions fixed.
Two girls and a boy, holding hands

2

As the tram rattled towards the city
she looked back towards the beach and saw
her two girls and a boy staring at the flat grey water of the Gulf,
staring, not playing on the sand
still holding hands, together,
hovering in that other life, just out of reach.
The summer sun roasting the sand, gulls hiding in shady corners
at the going home time of day,
when mothers children – gather, shake sand off towels,
call to their girls and boys, shading eyes against the glittery sun.

3

She'd left Glenelg years ago
but it would never abandon her.
She grew up here, she'd married here,
her mother and her sister still living in Alison street
in the house crouching behind the cypress hedge, and morning glory,
winding around the veranda like a promise,
with flowers like little blue trumpets she thought as a child.
This is where she'd always see her missing children, here and everywhere.
Two girls and a boy, she would see them,
suddenly appearing in a crowd,
outside David Jones in the Mall,
or down by the Torrens feeding swans,
not always holding hands but together at least.
Two girls and a boy, present yet absent too.

4

She'd lost them, not all at once, but one by one,
one girl at home in the garden,
pain knocking her to the ground,
she fell into the poppy bed, their stalks snapping like dry bones.
A girl and a boy she lost at the hospital in North Terrace,
where muscular roots of Moreton Bay figs
creep like invading troops from the Botanic Gardens, next door.
There her blood stained the white starched sheets,
hot under lights,
that tortured with relentless questions,
where nurses' voices murmured dove-like
and trolleys squeaked on scuffed lino.

5

She was never surprised to see them,
but shocked to see them growing – without her,
looking calmly away from her, not needing her
as if her own memories of them growing inside her
had been enough to sustain them forever.
And now as she returns to her river town beyond the hills
to her two boys
everywhere she knows she'll always see
her two girls and a boy.

Still Waiting

I have no answers why
we must say goodbye.
I cannot comprehend
that our embrace
must end.
Not in thunderous rage
or quiet hurt
but solemnly
like a sunset
or a morning's early light,
inevitable and bright
and soft like rain,
yet sharp with pain,
knowing we will not begin again.

Warnings

Warnings in the night,
and shadows like acid.
There's something moving deep inside
too deep to be removed
by surgeons with anonymous masks,
raiding bodies for their vital organs
and selling them on international markets.

Something has stolen my soul away,
left me like an empty tomb.

Wings echo in my soul,
a bird trapped in a room
beating itself to death slowly
against the glass of its own reflection,
flapping against the window of its trapped self
and with closing eyes…
…sees its closing eyes.

One goodbye

My lover has brought me to the station.
The sun is setting and the air is golden
we speak of trains shunting back and forth
soft words shunt between us
air caressing
pausing in and around our phrases.

He kisses me goodbye.
I put my bag in the carriage.
lean in the open doorway.
He stands on the platform facing me.
I say something about 50s films,
Lauren Bacall, Spencer Tracy.
Weren't they always leaving each other on trains?
Am I Bacall or Tracy?
I look up.
A honeyeater with russet breast
is calling from the top of the gum
above my lover's head
poking though the scarlet gum flower.

This is our moment of farewell, of separation
yet a moment of sudden intimacy.
Instead we examine the time
dropping its numbers on the platform clock.
How many minutes till our lives disengage?

We haven't been separated for a long time.
Sometimes I long to be separate,
times of argument, annoyance, misunderstanding.
Not now, not as it is about to happen

The train begins to move.
Our farewell words kiss in midair,
clumsy, inadequate.
The train is moving too quickly now,
suddenly he is gone from my sight.
Instead an old corrugated-iron fence flashes by.
I sit in the carriage
The dying sun shines on the dusty window
My eyes can see nothing outside.
Will I cry?
The train moves on now past an oval
Sprinklers dust the air with wet jewels
I'm going on a journey
I'm alone, not a couple now.
The train moves on through an evening painted with sadness.
Is this what love is?

In the steps of Eugenio

1

A man walks down a path,
a disappearing sort of path,
maybe a path going nowhere,
but a path we can't avoid.
I'm bright-eyed and just arrived in 1972,
nervous days, always the smell of Martial Law.

2

You're a tenant farmer,
snared by unjust landlords,
lockstep with Church and State,
they hate how you resist them.

3

That first day we met, your ragged shirt,
under your nails, dirt, your feet bare,
left mud prints on my stair,
that you never saw,
your mind on unjust law,
children dying without care.

4

Now I call that memory back
as a tide-rush up a beach,
I'll not forget
you leaning at the table just on dusk,
your hands sketched plans in air,
and all you ever asked of me
was friendship.

5

Fast forward on the days
you stand in court with unbowed head,
the judge complaining, looking down at me,
'Who is this foreign, meddling priest?'

6

Have you ever followed footprints on a beach,
tried to fit your feet to someone else's tread,
examined each step, scruff, skip or twist,
each print a trace of hope of fear, regret?
Who owns these steps we follow on so blindly?

7

Your steps move on from court to goal,
no crime but locked up just the same
So I brought books into your cell,
King's *Why we can't wait*
ignited fire in that small space
then baton-like passed back to me
its pages stained by a farmer's labouring hands.

8

King's words burned on the page for you
His letter from Birmingham goal proclaimed
'I am here because injustice lives here'
Your eyes alight repeating,
'oppressed cannot remain oppressed forever.'

9

For a moment you hesitate, contained
in that small space of hope,
released you broke free,
looked back just once and smiled,
me struggling still to match my
feet into the tracks you'd left behind.

10

Unused paths soon vanish,
un-followed footsteps fade.
We rush to remember that place, that time,
the saved places in our hearts,
the places we can never revisit,
spaces where we once lingered,
the friends who walked with us
who made us who we are.

Saved now for all our future remembering

Exclusion

Keep clear at all times
No parking
Stay away

1

It's the shadows we notice first,
options narrowing, a fading of light, a rejected idea,
then walls climb brick by brick.
Soon there are places in the mind
where light no longer falls and shadows gather.

In the past our walls had drawbridges and boiling oil was poured
from parapets to keep out what we could not understand.
These days we use firewalls and passwords or body searches at
airports to protect our lifestyle choices, to guard what we
have earned by our sweat, hard work and share portfolios.

Keep clear at all times
No parking
Stay away

2

In 1788 there were no passwords or firewalls,
no body searches at Botany Bay,
no coast guard turning back the First Fleet.
We all crept in under the cover of our whiteness.
The country lay open *terra nullius,*
terra nullius! terra firma! terra incognita!
Now the war on terror, the war on drugs,
the war on anything that threatens – terror australis –
we're an island secure unto ourselves, and
girt by sea, we exclude any who can't walk on water.
We decide who comes to this country
and the circumstances in which they come,
Australia forever off the asylum map.

Keep clear at all times
No parking
Stay away

3

Egg tempera lasts a very long time,
but exclusion has a longer history.
Here's Giotto in the 1300s inventing Renaissance wall graffiti,
cracking eggs and painting the *Last Judgement* on walls in Padua,
a medieval anarchist with spraycan warning of the crash.
Behind his back, famines and plagues ate up the working classes
and recessions and depressions spawned bankers
and other 14th century wankers,
with their hedge funds and their sub prime loans.

Keep clear at all times
No parking
Stay away

4

Yet behind our walls we choose small words
fold them, trim and shape them,
then propel our messages through breaches to the world outside.
Some lift and soar with hope
though most plunge lifeless to the earth ignored
or wander like lonely, unread emails in cyberspace.
But a few find rest in unexpected hearts, catch fire and blaze awhile,
disperse the shadows for a time and if there are enough
they rock the earth and walls do fall and streets of walls fall loudest.

Keep clear at all times
No parking
Stay away

5

Words scale walls, words burrow through walls,
words do pierce walls,
words weaken walls and in the end walls fear words
and walls fall down.

O Res Mirabilis

The smell of men
distilled desire
the raunch
the heat of lips
their whimpering cries
their prayers to god –
this sweet symphony of flesh
falls flat on ears
of haloed saints

Misunderstanding Good Friday

That Good Friday
we walked down the road
not towards Golgotha
but down McHenry street
to Holy Redeemer church –
no crowds baying for blood here
just us and our cat
that sometimes followed
all the way to Mass,
no Temple curtain rent in two,
just a memory of incense,
sombre saints veiled
in purple and
hot cross buns in the oven
on returning home.

The nails through the hands
& feet,
came later.

Life is

Life is
a journey through
the neglected gardens of
my childhood –
roses waiting to
be pruned
until you
assembled the pieces of
a telescope
magnetically
and I wait
patiently with tears
to peer into
remembrances
of god's own memory

Friendly Fire

Those years in Melbourne
when blood was

                              poison

the walls of

                              our hearts
                              caved in,

destroyed by phallic friendly fire –
the rooms of our youthful dreams
laid open

                              to the teeth

of premature winters

Our calendars pencilled black
with rendezvous

                              of funeral dates

They slipped away

                              those men

like soldiers on the Somme front line
We felt the bullets
thud into lovers

                              their bodies

filling up with lead
who'd left us minutes ere
our lives

                              cooled

from their embrace

The call of the Border

When murder
knocks on the door at night.

When home
is a ticking time-bomb

When despair
is all that is left to eat

Only fools
snatch their children from sleep,
secrete them on boats
in the dark

Only fools
leave homes still on fire
murdered loved ones unburied

Only fools heed the call of the border
like migrating birds
oblivious to borders

The true border
lies within the soul
halfway between courage
and extermination.

The falcon

(To Christ our Lord)

The day the cardinal went
                      to goal
cathedral cupolas cracked
church walls crumpled
bishops bled
                      from every orifice
and
all the saints' statues
wept together
                      in harmony

a falcon plunging low,
feathers a Japanese fan
cooling the air,
tethered me puppet-like
with invisible strings
– a Manley Hopkins Windhover
                      mastering air
or,
– ah, my dear –
was it the Holy Spirit
                      resummoned
                      to triage
all we wounded souls?

Tenderness

tenderness of patient minds
love of absent ones
light at dusk
a child's delight –
all these like lightning
spark
the life within

Still around

When we returned home
from your funeral
I found some ashes
stuck to the bottom of the container
inscribed 'honouring a life'

Your Peter Sellers' impressions
kept interrupting my thoughts
so I bought a
Eucalyptus Woodwardii
watering with your
washed out ashes –
dedicated to thoroughness
as always

It flowered last summer
after four years
brushes of scarlet
tickling blue sky days

You visit some nights
still insisting on wearing
those green shoes

Close encounters with headlines

On July 17th 2014
why were the sunflower fields
of Ukraine
littered with *Silly Milly Moo*
backpacks of children,
the women of Hrabove

laying flowers with tears?
On the same flight path
that day
was I unwrapping my inflight
citrus grilled chicken
narrowly missing
an encounter with a headline?

In 2002
crossing the bay
from Queenscliffe to Sorrento
the ferry bounced
in the *Tampa*'s wake
another narrow encounter
with a headline.

But in 1974
in the city of Ozamis
in the southern Philippines
I shook hands with a headline
Imelda Marcos hurling sweets
to refugee children
fleeing their burning homes

Some headlines
leave us floundering
in their wake
reverberating long after

We keep bouncing

My Acolyte Eyes

My acolyte eyes
follow men,
the grace of their
Caravaggio limbs
in motion
My lips tremble
with prayers
that their eyes
may fall upon me

I sing hymns
to their hair
wind-winnowed
like wheat

I adore the communion
of lips & tongues
like citrus-shock

I choose the vocabulary
of skin
ripe as an incense
cupped in their
thuribled thighs

If my desire
be called idolatry
then like Lucifer
I fall to earth gladly,
the Morning Star
of blasphemy

Lizard

A lizard runs through the grass
Like a spilled cup of tea
Static crackles from eyried boardrooms
According to the order of Melchisedech

Like a spilled cup of tea
Random thoughts are already tadpoles
According to the order of Melchisedech
While toads are still advancing

Random thoughts are already tadpoles
And some sinners do repent
While toads are still advancing
Climate cannot be denied forever

And some sinners do repent
Though cardinals wear the colour of blood
Climate cannot be denied forever
As long as brimstone is back in fashion

Though cardinals wear the colour of blood
Lizards favour frilly-collared necks
As long as brimstone is back in fashion
Like a spilled cup of tea

Disturbed by zinnias

Thrusting themselves
over bluestone walls
you blatant geometric exhibitionists
no soft pale roundness here
no delicate botanic understatement
just shouting 'Look at me!'

Bella Donna

Steel-sharp thrusting penis
from concrete earth

Once im-per-ceptible
now un-re-lent-less
androgenous buds
unfurling soft moist petals.

You beautiful woman
armed with your spear.

Wetlands

The day you left home
I drove to the wetlands
searching for egrets,
seeking out their persistent
faith in survival
their resistance to loss,
those patient *shui mo* egrets
held captive for thousands of years
then released from a Chinese screen
stabbing & spearing
determined to survive
until evening

Only when I returned home
and you were still gone
did I fall down,
poured out like water
flowing across wetlands
unstoppable

The McDonald's Car Park Massacre

Here in the car park of McDonald's
there's blood been spilt
hidden for now, still invisible,
not fresh blood
from gangs of young men
wearing inverted baseball caps and
bored insolence
but old-blood
almost-forgotten blood
seeped-into-the earth blood
but never-to-be-erased blood.

This blood of the Wathaurong
runs free at night
when city traffic lights
wink lonely signals
at each other
and the songs of the massacred
stack on one another like
piles of unwashed dishes,
before toppling into
forgetfulness

The ambiguity of hands

Hands
that stab or strangle
can cradle babies

What are we to make
of hands
that betray us?

Hands
can mend or end
a life
a punch
or surgeon's touch
it's just another pair
of hands

I still recall
my parents' hands
held tight
right
until the end

Mind the gap

When the very white train from Geelong
sidled into Tarneit station
people of African appearance
took two deep breaths
and got on board
no seats available
we passengers of white appearance
stared stolidly ahead
what could we do?
Seats were limited.

For your safety
please ensure
there is still sufficient racism available
when you disembark
at the platform.

Thank you for your attention.

Domesticated Violence

When men kill
their wives and partners
TV news crews invade suburbs with
neat lawns and succulent gardens
they interview neighbours
who grasp collars around their necks
for protection
'they always kept to themselves'
they say
eyes darting sideways and
'this is such a friendly neighbourhood'

In nearby streets
men close the curtains silently
to drown out the sobbing
of their wives

Holding on to the Bible

The air crackled with
an overload of irony & police sirens
the day the Leader stood
before the Church, shuttered and bulwarked
against our rage & disappointment

He held his Bible
        awkwardly
as if handling a baby with a crapped diaper
or a hot loaf of bread sliding
unexpectedly from the oven

When you called for Law & Order
were you calling down the gods of war
like reliable but overworked Mars
or was it Ares or Shiva?

Were you channelling those prophets
of revenge, Isaiah, Jeremiah & Elija
still suffering their own forms of PTSD ?

Your fingers did clutch those pages tight
lest errant words leak out – like
> *…Blessed are the peacemakers:*
> *for they shall be called the children of God.*

There's nothing like the whiff of tear gas
in the evening

Small matters

While sleek men
in comfortable suits
propose wars
that plough the fields
with blood and bone
of our young

While heads of state
and presidents inflate
and then explode
stern men plan coups
these men of iron and bronze
who shake the earth
make kingdoms tremble
their crackling static
spilling out of
eyried boardrooms –

twilight flashes across paddocks
a blue wren jogs in grass
a passing stranger smiles
mating humpbacks expand their repertoire
your beloved approaches across a room
you plant a tree with hope

These small things
these are the things that matter.

Hope

When I awoke this morning
that old god had gone AWOL
deities had scattered
like skittish ponies
the captain was hiding
in the lifeboat.

Does hope have a colour?
What song does it sing?
Is it pale umber
over burnt paddocks
or blue where ocean
kisses watercolour sky,
still waiting to dry?

Is hope a Bach sonata
heard nightly in balconied courtyards,
shadows athrill,
seduced by gardenia
or is it Black Sabbath
acrid with dust,
burning rubber
and a whiff of gasoline?

No,
hope is just
an acrobat
swinging on a high wire
out of reach
and
without a safety net.

After the surgery

1

In the morning
the girl who brings the tray
hopes the rain will
fill her tanks.

Later,
two cleaners
mopping round my bed
swap anecdotes
on snakes and bushfires.

At night
a nurse drops the water jug
and swears.

I feel the current
of their words
flow round me,
the loving arms
of Endone
weigh me down
for now.

Like the salmon and the gudgeon
I'm preparing to leap upstream
towards the daylight.

2

Those nights
held captive
by machine whirr and beep
she comes to me
my mother
that 1930s nurse
in starched white veil and smile
rechecking all my charts.

Breathe in love
and
breathe out fear.

3

The day I came home
from hospital
I watched a honeyeater
swinging upside down,
feasting on bottlebrush.

How fine the line between
disintegration
and euphoria.

Love letter to the Führer

Mein liebster Führer,
though you put a bullet
through your brain,
it wasn't all in vain
at last it's fine to hate again
though not yet on the scale
achieved by you.

Now the trials of Nürnberg
have faded,
mein Führer,
our leaders now can choose once more
those worth of the title
Herrenvolk.
It's just the
natural state of things returning
the white race once more
superior, it's proven.

So it's your
inevitable arrival
we now await,
glory incarnate,
mein Fuhrer.

An admirer

Self-portrait by Berthe Morisot

She lived a smudged existence
trapped in high-collar days
but boldly
while all about her (the world)
exploded in pinpricks of light
like a shattering windscreen
hit by a random stone,
that simple ping that pauses,
then splits into diamonded shards.

She kept her hands on the wheel
her foot to the floor
no Thelma and Louise escape for her
she wore her brooch of failure
bravely
as a badge of honour.

A Ghazal

Of the fruit I ate
The serpent beguiled me
But still I wait
The serpent beguiled me

I long for a meaning
Nights filled with snakes
In my mind there's a gate
The serpent beguiled me

My lips search for you
While I dream of your eyes
To search for love is my fate
The serpent beguiled me

I ache for your arms
The warmth of desire
I love but I hate
The serpent beguiled me

Once John's name meant
Beloved of them all
Now all I can state is
The serpent beguiled me

Know thyself

Without the beach
there is no sand.
Without the heat
there is no glass.
Without aluminium
There is no mirror
and
without the mirror
do I still exist?

So I look through
that glass darkly
I know only in part
then I shall fully know
and
be fully known.

Without that mirror
the sea eternal
will engulf us.

Acknowledgements

'Disturbed by Zinnias', January 2020, Red Room Poetry – https://redroomcompany.org/ poem/ new- shoots-public submissions/disturbed-zinnias/

'Under Construction', 'Misunderstanding Good Friday', November 2019, *Meniscus Literary Review* – https://www.meniscus.org.au/Vol_2.pdf

'After the Surgery', December 2019, *fourW thirty* Anthology

'Noumea Quartet', August 2019, Brain Drip – https://braind.rip/poetry/noumeaquartet

'As sand is', November 2019, *Poetry Matters*, Issue 37

'The call of the Border', July 2019, The Lake – http://www.thelakepoetry.co.uk/poetry/john-bartlett/

'Still Around', April 2019, Bluepepper – https://bluepepper.blogspot.com/2019/04/new-poetry-by-john-bartlett.html

'The Blue', 'Shame', 'Danger', November 2018, Poetry Pacific – http://poetrypacific.blogspot.eom.au/

'Barre-Warre – From the Hills to the Sea' – http://disappearing.com.au/poem/barre-warre-from-the-hills-to-the-sea/

'47 Alison Street' – 1994, Red Room Poetry – https://redroomcompany-dot-yammtrack.appspot.com/Redirect?ukey=11XPnv19AmD4jp3RzR,gwOLZSDSGK-iAJJuS-Tjhn494-0&key=YAMMID-12596569&link=http%3A%2F%2Fdisappearing.com.au%2Fpoem%2F47-alison-street-1994-john- bartlett%2F

'Night', November 2017, Bluepepper – http://bluepepper.blogspot.com.au/2017/11/new-poetry-by-johnbartlett.html

'Rewind', November 2017, Right Now – http://rightnow.org.au/

'Surf Coast – Boxing Day 2015', *Otway Life Almanac*, 2018

'Drifting', Right Now, November 2017 – http://rightnow.org.au/poetry/drifting/

'I lie down', 'Apocalypse', 'Jacaranda', 'Listening for the past', April 2018, *Meniscus Literary Review*

'Manus', March 2018, Right Now – http://rightnow.org.au/poetry/manuspoetry/

'Litanies on the Homeward Road', 'Saying the Rosary', May 2018, InDaily poet's corner – https://indaily.com.au/tag/poets-corner/

'The Blue', March 2018, Bluepepper – https://bluepepper.blogspot.com.au/

'Plastic World', May 2018, Porridge Magazine – https://porridgemagazine.com/2018/05/31/one-poem-john-bartlett/

'Mistakes', Cordite, August 2018 – http://cordite.org.au

'Red Brick Wall', 'Absence', 'Presence', November 2018, *Orbis Quarterly International Literary Journal*

'Surprised by Love', 'Herons', 'The Wedding Dress', September 2018, InDaily poet's corner – https://indaily.com.au/arts-and-culture/books-andpoetry/2018/09/26/poems-of-love-and-loss/

'Some God', from *Love and Fear: A Poetry Anthology*, Artary Project Space

Poems Appearing in *The Arms of Men* (Melbourne Poets Union, 2019

'Wetlands'
'Drifting'
'Last light'
'Once'
'Apocalypse'
'Grace still hovers'
'Damaged angels'
'Manus'
'Rewind'
'The Angelus'
'Saying the Rosary'
'Surprised by love'
'The uncertainty of men'
'Awake at 3 a.m.'
'I lie down'
'What a piece of work is man'
'My acolyte eyes'
'Listening for the past'
'47 Alison Street, 1984'
'Jacaranda'
'Remembering Michael'
'Litanies on the homeward road'

www.ingramcontent.com/pod-product-compliance
Lightning Source LLC
Chambersburg PA
CBHW070916080526
44589CB00013B/1314